PEACOCK DREAMING: THE WISDOM OF FLOWERS

Anne McCormack

First published in Nelson, New Zealand, 2017

Edited by Matt Mostyn: www.mattmostyn.com
Photos by Anne McCormack
The Author may be contacted at anne.mccormack7@gmail.com
www.peacockdreaming.co.nz

Balboa Press books may be ordered through booksellers or by contacting:

Balboa Press
A Division of Hay House
1663 Liberty Drive
Bloomington, IN 47403
www.balboapress.com
1 (877) 407-4847

ISBN: 978-1-5043-0776-5 (sc)
ISBN: 978-1-5043-0777-2 (e)

Print information available on the last page.

Balboa Press rev. date: 06/06/2017

BALBOA. PRESS
A DIVISION OF HAY HOUSE

Acknowledgement

With thanks to the lovely Leasa Anderson for her support, encouragement and faith in my abilities to make this book happen. Thank you to my beautiful family and friends. Thank you to all of my teachers. Thank you to Mother Nature. Thank you to my peahen and peacock. Whilst you have flown across the other side of the valley, you continue to inspire and teach me. You will always remain in my heart.

Contents

Introduction

My handsome boy

Many years ago, I would regularly attend the local Spiritualist Church where I lived in Sydney, Australia. During mediumship training and meditation circles, one of my favourite exercises was flower reading. We would each bring a flower in a paper or plastic bag, which was dropped into a basket as we arrived.

The basket would then be passed around the circle, and each of us would choose a bag we felt drawn to. The theory went that the flower held the energy of the person who had picked it – and so any information gleaned from the flower would be pertinent to the person who'd placed it in the basket.

It always amazed me how much information came through. Whilst doing these readings, many newcomers would start off uncertain – but after looking at the flower, and describing how it looked, certain attributes became apparent, which could often be linked with a feeling or an action the flower-picker had been dealing with.

For me, feelings and colours bring forth a lot of information. Being strongly clairsentient (that is, I feel the emotions and feelings of those around me, whether they be human, plant or animal), and thanks to my metaphysical training, colours contain strong meaning.

I remember the first time I read a flower, its colours seemed to be extraordinarily luminescent. While holding it, I felt feelings and physical pains that were not mine – and yet when I let go of the flower, those feelings dissipated. As I take in their delicate intricacies, flowers lead me on an incredible journey of discovery. For me, flower reading is a powerful exercise, and one which never ceases to amaze me.

Where Did The Wisdom of Flowers Come From?

Over the last few years, I've delighted in using photography to capture the beauty of plants and flowers. Their magnificence seem to call out to me through the lens of my camera. I realised that it's possible to utilise photographs of flowers in much the same way as we'd done through flower reading all those years ago.

During meditations, I would hold a photograph of a flower or plant, and words would come to me, as if the foliage was speaking to me, providing words of guidance and gentle reassurance.

The intention of Peacock Dreaming: Wisdom Of Flowers is that in times of turmoil, you can randomly select an image to provide you with comfort, transforming your troubles into a clearer perspective, and helping you to move forward.

The mission with these images is to encourage you to trust your intuition, helping you realise that you're always guided and supported. Some of what you see, feel and hear may not make sense to you. Simply trust that you're being shown these things for a reason. Do not stem the flow of words that come from your mouth, or the thoughts that come to you, for fear of not making sense.

My greatest wish for you in using Peacock Dreaming: Wisdom Of Flowers is that you'll find a way to understand your own process, whilst strengthening your intuitive muscle and nurturing compassion toward others, so that you may venture forward responsibly toward your goals, with love in your heart.

Magic happens!

The Influence Of The Peacocks

My beautiful peahen

The significance of peacocks is deeply personal for me, and it's something that has taken me completely by surprise.

Back in December 2014, my partner Geoff and I decided to get ourselves a couple of peacocks. We liked the idea of the birds free-ranging across our country abode. While many might consider chickens to be a more practical choice, we felt that if we were going to have birds shitting on our concrete, we'd be more forgiving about cleaning up after them if they were pretty to look at! As it turns out, this shallow sentiment turned into something much more soulful and heartfelt, as the peacocks brought such laughter and amusement into the house with their daily visits to the living room window. We especially enjoyed it when the peacock would posture, vibrate and display, while the peahen stonily ignored his advances!

Yet over time, Geoff and I noticed that both birds were increasingly enjoying the company of the other animals in our top paddock. They began venturing from the step of the cottage (where they would admire themselves in the reflection of the glass door), into the paddock, amongst the sheep, horses and cows.

And then, just as the old year ended and a new one began, they were spooked by an overly-inquisitive cow by the name of 'Coffee', and took off across the valley.

Double Trouble

It was our peacock who went first. He'd been picking at the grass just below the hedge, when Coffee the cow bumbled along and gave him a fright. He flew up into the pine trees below the house, to a loud bang, crash and a squawk (he was never very good at judging distance, and always seemed to aim right for any obstacle in his path). And then he vanished.

Over the next couple of days, we searched high and low. I would try to tune into his energy to see if he was okay (I'd learnt how to do this in the development circle meditations many years before, when we practised remote viewing). We went walking through the pine forest to see if we could see him hiding beneath the fallen trees. He was nowhere to be found.

A few days later, he'd still not returned home – but then, one morning, in the distance, we suddenly heard him call out to the peahen. It sounded like he was across the other side of the valley. We felt relieved that at least he was ok.

Even though her beau was elsewhere, our lovely little peahen still seemed content at home. She would spend the mornings having a dust bath as I tended to my vegetable garden. In the afternoons, whilst I was away at work, she would spend time with Geoff and our dog, Ridge, down in the paddock.

It was a week after the flight of the peacock that Coffee the cow struck again. She suddenly broke into a rather uncoordinated run down the hill, part curious about the peahen, and also eager to see whether Geoff was carrying his white bucket full of paddock nuts. The poor bird took flight with a squawk, and a panicked flap of her wings, and flew away.

I missed their presence in the garden, and was worried for their wellbeing, but was heartened when our neighbours across the valley told us they'd heard peacock sounds not too far away. I couldn't stop thinking about them, though, and prayed they were safe. I tried tuning in to them, but didn't getting any strong feelings. Yet I had an inner knowing that they were fine. Three days after the peahen left, I had a really vivid dream, one that I realised the significance of days later, once I'd had an opportunity to process it.

In the dream, whilst tracking the peacocks, I ended up in what I felt to be urban Sydney. From my experiences living there 20 years earlier, I felt wary and anxious. The peacocks, while happy to see me, were preoccupied with exploring their new surroundings. Like an overprotective parent, I followed them through buildings full of people, making sure they weren't getting into harm's way. I wanted to contact my parents to let them know where I was, but I kept losing my iPhone and iPad.

I followed the birds to a construction site, and climbed some scaffolding, where I found them roosting up high, on a steel member. I lost them once again, but managed to track them to the front of another building, where there was a beautiful rose garden. Other, much older peacocks with beautiful eye feathers were there, too. I tried phoning Mum, but there was no reception.

At this point I woke up, feeling a strange mixture of sorrow and peace, and a desire to piece together the message of this surreal dream.

After meditation, contemplation and reading, I realised the dream was showing me where I was at emotionally, and my hopes and fears concerning the launch of my photography and spiritual work. My obsession with the peacocks was telling me that now was the time to acknowledge those aspirations within myself, and to act on them.

After qualifying as an aromatherapist and remedial massage therapist in Sydney all those years ago, I'd begun working professionally in clinics around the city. With every day of massage, my sensitivity grew, along with my thirst for knowledge. My longing to understand this new sensitivity led me to study parapsychology and metaphysics. As part of my studies, I would meditate, both between appointments and at my development circles. It reached the point where my whole life was one meditation – and I didn't cope very well with the real world, and all its responsibilities (which is not something I'm particularly proud of, or wish to make excuses for).

To cut a long and complicated story short, after a brief stay at a Tibetan Buddhist monastery in Queensland, I decided that I needed to take control of my life in a rather more conscious fashion. I needed to be in a place that nurtured and supported me, rather than somewhere that sapped me of energy. Brisbane was just the place, being affordable to live, with a slower, gentler pace, which would allow me to process everything and ground myself.

With my new occupation in the construction industry, my spiritual world gradually transformed. Initially I wore my spiritual self quite literally on my sleeve. I didn't subscribe to the corporate wardrobe, sticking instead with my purple and pink tie-dye combinations (which, I must say, brightened up the taupe and charcoal-hued corporate surroundings no end!). I talked openly about communicating with Spirit, about energy healing and aromatherapy – and while many colleagues were interested and welcoming, my managers were for the most part slightly less enamoured. One manager even left in the top drawer of my desk a copy of the Bible, with excerpts from Deuteronomy highlighted and underlined (quite confronting, as the suggestion seemed to be that I was doing something evil, even though my intent was straight from the heart). Additionally, management seemed to resist taking me seriously enough to trust me with more challenging work tasks.

I gradually learnt that conforming externally (that is, keeping my spiritual self private) was the key to earthbound advancement. Managers started to focus more on my potential, encouraging me to go back to university, and I was rewarded with new job opportunities. I wanted to support myself, own a home and be accepted and respected for my contributions in the workplace. Over the next ten years I lived in Brisbane, followed by five years in Christchurch, New Zealand – and I experienced romantic love and the challenges that comes with relationships, with the transition from the 'lust phase' into unconditional love. We bought and sold a little 'renovators delight'. I took on the responsibility of caring for my partner through his lengthy illness, learning how to process his medication-driven mood swings and depression, while maintaining my love for him. I earned myself a role as a Project Manager, and savoured the feeling of guiding building projects to completion, to the delight of satisfied clients.

Throughout this time, the desire to practice alternative healing never left me. Whenever I could, I went away on retreat to work through the levels of training for Ka Huna Massage, a form of Polynesian bodywork. In New Zealand, I started photography, which became a healing modality of sorts, facilitating clarity and a sense of peace during difficult times. I toyed constantly with the idea of diving back into healing work, but there was a constant feeling that my path would not only include massage, aromatherapy and energy healing work; I felt there was something more to it.

Analysing that dream of the peacocks, I spent much time questioning 'what', 'why' and 'how'. The scene in the rose garden, being surrounded by peacocks, the message that came to me was one of incredible love. The peacocks took me back to a time when I first opened up to my spiritual gifts, which was a truly magical, exciting time for me. However, it was also a time of significant challenges, which were often quite brutal for a sensitive and immature young adult. It was a very special, yet scary place to be.

I realised that the part where I lost my phone and iPad represented me being scattered. Back in those Sydney days, I spent most of my time in meditation, out in the ether. I wasn't coping well with the real world. The message was that I need to consolidate my energies. I was shown that being distracted, and treading a path that took me away from my original goals, was a constant challenge.

With regard to the buildings, while following the peacocks through the lower level floors, I realised this was a reflection of my earthbound issues, like safety and security. And climbing the scaffolding related to the surge of new energy and ambition, and a renewed sense of confidence. The message was loud and clear. I had a lot of work to do before the building was complete – but my foundations and structure were strong, and built to last.

Today, I stand on the precipice of one of the most thrilling journeys of my life. Spiritually I am heading back to a time of revisiting and honing my intuitive gifts and magic, combining them with new skills and talents I had not known about all those years ago. Now it's time for me to approach life in a more grounded fashion, while taking actual positive steps toward achieving a dream I'm perpetually drawn toward.

The peacocks, and that powerful dream symbolise the 'what', 'why' and 'how' of my present reality. In fact, it was the peacock dream that prompted me to write this book.

I hope that in turn, you'll find the inspiration to follow your own 'peacock dreams' to fruition – and I hope also that these flowers will bring you a beautiful sense of clarity, comfort and guidance, just as they've done for me.

This peacock was sitting in a tree when I visited Wharariki, near Golden Bay, on New Zealand's South Island.

Significance Of The Number 42

Peacock Dreaming: Wisdom of Flowers consists of 42 images of flowers and plants. Numerologically, 42 is a very special number for anyone seeking guidance, while wishing to be nurtured. It's about harmony, idealism, family, relationships and focus, with a pinch of responsibility as you shine your light toward your own destiny.

For those 'Hitchhikers Guide To The Galaxy' fans, the number 42 also represents the answer to the 'Ultimate Question in Life, the Universe and Everything'.

Peacock Dreaming Flower Wisdom

The key to working with Peacock Dreaming: Wisdom of Flowers is to first centre yourself and focus your intent. Close your eyes, and take a deep breath. In your mind, reflect on the question or life situation you need clarity on. Then, when you feel drawn to do so, open the book at a random page.

Before reading the words accompanying the image, take some time to ground yourself. Begin by envisaging yourself as a tree, with roots growing deep into the earth. Then imagine a column of white light pouring down through the top of your head, down your spine and legs into your feet, and into the ground below. Imagine that column of light travelling deep into the earth, until it reaches a pool of pink light. Now imagine your 'roots' sucking up the pink light, drawing it up into your body with every inhalation. Each time you exhale, imagine the pink light moving out into your auric field, the area surrounding your physical body. This mini-meditation helps to ground you, and to tap into your limitless pool of unconditional love.

Now look deeply into the image of the flower. What are the first feelings, words, and thoughts that come to you? Write them down, without judging or analysing them.

Further insights on reading flower images can be accessed in the closing chapters of this book.

Understanding

WE ALL CRAVE TO BE UNDERSTOOD
AND ACCEPTED FOR WHO WE ARE.

WE CAN MANIFEST THIS DESIRE
ONE PERSON AT A TIME.

TAKE THE TIME TO LISTEN
TO ANOTHER PERSON
WITH AN OPEN HEART,
AND WATCH THEM DO
THE SAME FOR YOU.

The world is full of differing opinions and objectives, conflicting interests, and opposing agendas. We all strive to be understood and accepted – yet fully understanding another person often comes from being able to place yourself in their shoes and feel what they're feeling. We can all sometimes make weird and even unsavoury choices – and it's easy to judge ourselves, and others quite harshly in these moments, deciding we, or they are unworthy of love and acceptance. Yet a little compassion and empathy can shed light on those underlying motivations.

We don't need to passively accept the crimes and misdeeds of others. However, it's far from healthy to hold on to the anger, mistrust, and sorrow we experience as a result of these their actions. These emotional responses keep our hearts closed. A more enlightened approach means acknowledging that their actions are a consequence of their own suffering. Wish them peace and blessings, and let them go.

Trust

DON'T HANG ON TO THE PAST.
TRUST YOURSELF TO LET GO.
KNOW THAT YOU WILL
BE SAFE FROM HARM.
YOUR LANDING WILL BE
SOFT AND GENTLE,
YOU DON'T NEED TO FORCE IT.
JUST LET IT HAPPEN!

Fight or flight: it's a primal and wholly understandable reaction. Sometimes, life's twists and turns can manoeuvre us into treacherous currents. Our head tells us the canoe will tip over, and we'll fall overboard. Our body tenses, anticipating the worst, expending energy on fear, instead of directing it toward something more fruitful.

Expecting the worst outcome closes you off to support, and prevents you appreciating people and situations for what they are. Living in fear shuts down your intuition, and blocks spiritual guidance.

Instead, be like an autumn leaf about to drop from the tree. Don't assume the landing will be hard. Remember that when you expect the worst, that's what you'll likely attract. Envisage a gentle flight, delivering you safely and securely where you need to go.

Commitment

When you commit to
another person,
you do not need to give away
your uniqueness and values.
Instead commit to
unconditional love.
This commitment
is sustainable!

When our hearts and souls are enlivened by excitement and passion, we're able to do whatever it takes to achieve our dreams and overcome any obstacle. Determination and tenacity keep us moving toward our goals – yet it's just as important to apply that same passion, fervour and tenacity towards personal relationships.

Perhaps your sense of commitment is not quite as strong as it could be. Perhaps you're feeling depleted, or taken for granted on some level. Perhaps you even feel a little used. What's holding you back from feeling enlivened by your relationship? Are you driven by passion, or by a sense of duty, responsibility or obligation? What will it take for you to show up 100%?

It's time to give yourself a break. If you're taking another's responsibilities on to your own shoulder, now's the time hand back that responsibility, with loving kindness. Reflect on what you enjoy about your more successful relationships. What makes you feel energised?

Remember, humans are more resilient than we give ourselves credit for. We can work through the most difficult situations, even when pain or unpleasantness spring up along the way. Break down the journey into small pieces. Where there is a fork in the path, or a decision to be made, turn within, and ask for guidance.

Present

It is when we are wounded and scared that we are tempted by the path of medication and avoidance.

Learn to live in the here and now. Take the time to heal. Be honest with yourself. You'll be guided in the moment along the path that best serves you.

We miss so much of our lives. We run to and from appointments. We're planning our futures. We're busy keeping busy. We forget to stop, to observe ourselves and the world around us. We miss out on so much beauty, because we're far too busy to take time to appreciate it.

This was my reality for many years. I have always been busy. I've filled my head with so many thoughts that there's been no room to appreciate my life, and the beauty that surrounds me.

It wasn't t until I reached 41 and moved to New Zealand that I was guided towards changing this. During a particularly emotionally challenging period, I began taking evening walks, getting out into nature. I started noticing the variety of flowers in bloom, and the colours of the hills and the rocks, the magnificent views. My mindset shifted to "how lucky am I?" as I took in these sights. I began capturing these sights on my iPhone and sharing them on social media. Others reminded me how lucky I was to be living amongst such beauty.

I took a trip to my home town of Adelaide, where I kept my habit of taking walks, and taking photographs, and I found that beauty followed me around. My Adelaide friends restated their envy, not realising this beauty was right on their doorstep! They just needed to take the time to see it.

There is so much to be thankful for. We just need to take a few moments each day to acknowledge it.

Spirit

SPIRIT IS ALWAYS WITH YOU,
GUIDING AND REASSURING YOU.
YOU ARE NEVER ALONE.

What is this 'Spirit' I speak of so much? Spirit is the soul essence of those who have gone before you.

We are more than just the physical bodies we inhabit, and the life lessons we experience. We are all a part of the collective consciousness. We learn from one another, and we collectively develop and evolve. In essence, you are spirit.

That gut instinct... that the little voice in our conscience warning us not to do something… the messages we get where the written or spoken word resonates so strongly and sends chills up our arms... these are all the ways in which Spirit communicates.

Certain lessons were predetermined before we were born – and we have a number of spirit guides, who continually assist us on our path. We might ignore our intuition, or fail to seek help or guidance. Nevertheless, our guides are always there, waiting to be of service. They orchestrate energies, and they bring events into alignment, to aid our growth and wellbeing.

Take the time to focus your energies on communicating with your spirit guides at least once a day. You may not hear them – but you may feel sensations, or receive visual messages. Some of us are naturally sensitive to touch, sight, smell, or words. Our spirit guides will utilise those tools. Tune in, and listen to their messages.

Listen

LISTEN TO YOUR HEART,
THE WORDS,
BODY LANGUAGE AND
ACTIONS OF OTHERS.
YOU WILL RECEIVE
THE INFORMATION
AND WISDOM
YOU SEEK.

Sometimes we generate too much noise. Mind chatter and overthinking stop us being able to hear the messages, or see the signs. Forever on a treadmill, we fall into pre-emptive patterns. We over-anticipate, trying to always stay one step ahead. We're busy people-pleasing. We're busy being busy.

Just stop! Listen to what you're being shown. Notice how your heart feels. Dispassionately observe any negative feelings, like dread or anxiety, instead of being consumed by them. Notice the synchronous events occurring in your life.

Doing this, you will better comprehend and interpret the meaning and motives that come your way. You'll misinterpret less, and trust more.

Blessings

I KNOW IT'S DIFFICULT TO
SEE THIS SOMETIMES,
BUT YOU HAVE A LOT TO
CELEBRATE TODAY.
YOU MAY SEE LIFE THROUGH
THE EYES OF YOUR SORROW,
BUT THERE ARE MANY THINGS
TO FEEL BLESSED FOR.
SEEING THIS BEAUTY
DOESN'T TAKE AWAY YOUR
PAIN AND SUFFERING –
BUT TAKING TIME TO
ACKNOWLEDGE
THESE BLESSINGS
MAY TAKE THE EDGE OFF A LITTLE.

During even the roughest of times, our lives still contain blessings worth acknowledging. These reminders can salve our wounds and soothe our troubled hearts, even if just momentarily.

Our animals can sense our pain, offering the comfort of their presence, reminding us that we're not alone. A walk in the park, in nature, can provide respite when we take the time to appreciate the intricate beauty of plants and flowers.

There are blessings to be found in most situations. It's so easy for us to be drawn into the drama and tragedy of a situation that we often forget to acknowledge the more positive aspects.

Life is magical! The more we begin to acknowledge the blessings in our lives, the more those blessings will become apparent. When we can appreciate the better aspects of our circumstances, the more we begin to wake up every day and say 'how did I become so lucky', instead of 'why me'.

Playfulness

SOMETIMES WE TAKE LIFE
FAR TOO SERIOUSLY.
LAUGHING AND ENJOYING
THE MOMENT
IS THE KEY TO ENLIGHTENING
OUR SPIRIT.
SPEND TIME WITH ANIMALS
OR CHILDREN
TO REACQUAINT YOURSELF WITH
YOUR OWN INNER CHILD.

Nurture the playful heart of your inner child and you'll find the antidote to stress and anxiety. Playfulness enables us to take a break from day-to-day stresses, and gives our minds some time out.

Notice when you're feeling tired, bored, anxious, sad or angry, and take some time – even just a few minutes – to engage in fun and general silliness.

If you're unable to escape from your workplace (and so long as you're not in a meeting at the time), you might break out the dance moves, or make up a song about your frustration.

Often laughter (other people's, as well as your own) can break down and dissipate that dense stress energy we sometimes emit. Your laughter may even give way to a few tears. That's just as helpful. Like laughter, tears also are a form of release from stress.

A light-hearted take on life adds light when there is darkness. Nothing seems quite so bad when you can lighten your own mood, and the moods of others.

Happiness

HAPPINESS
IS ACCEPTING THE
WAY YOU ARE
AND LOVING WHO YOU ARE
UNCONDITIONALLY.

Happiness really does come from the inside. If you seek it from external sources, like people or possessions, the fulfilment will be fleeting, and you'll be left feeling empty.

Try focusing on the present. Take the time to go for a walk. Study the trees, the flowers, the skyline, the colours all around you. Greet the people you encounter with a smile. Take the time to savour a lick of your favourite ice cream, or the melodies of your favourite music. Feel yourself being moved by the little things around you.

Put aside for a moment your goals and aspirations, and just be in the moment with your experiences. Really feel your blessings, and feel how lucky you are that you can enjoy life's simple pleasures.

Happiness is infectious. It's a self-perpetuating force that goes from strength to strength. All you need to do is find and appreciate life's simple pleasures in every moment.

Connectedness

YOU BELONG.
OPEN YOUR HEART TO THE WORLD AROUND YOU.
SEEK OUT THE COMPANY OF LIKE-MINDED OTHERS.
THE UNIVERSAL LAW OF ATTRACTION IS AT PLAY.

Somebody may be absent right now – but it doesn't mean they're not with you. Those dearest to our hearts live there for eternity. Know that even though you might feel alone, you never really are. Remember that you're surrounded by people, plants, animals and energies that resonate, and can help to uplift you.

Every living thing is supported with food, water, oxygen and nutrients. Animals are just as sensitive as we are to human emotions and vulnerabilities. My life on a small farm in rural New Zealand has taught me to become more attuned to the world around me. I walk up to trees, touch their leaves and receive their insights. I feel the anxiety, fear and love of my animals, helping me to radiate more love and care towards them – and in turn, they respond.

People may be pushing your buttons right now, exacerbating your stress levels with their gestures and words. It's okay to take time out by yourself. In nature you can find compassionate healing, with no need to explain yourself. Seek out the places that provide a feeling of gentleness and connectedness that soothes your soul.

Grief

ALLOW YOURSELF TIME,
FOR THE TEARS WILL PASS.
TEARS CLEANSE.
A TIME OF RENEWAL WILL FOLLOW
WHEN YOU ARE READY.

Sometimes loss seems hard to bear. Tears are shed, and emotions are raw. At this time, we are at our most vulnerable.

Healing takes time, and the pace at which this happens varies from person to person. Everyone has a unique process of healing to go through. The journey is dependent on, and influenced by our relationships with ourselves, and those around us. When another tries to place a timeframe on your grief, remember this often about their own feelings of discomfort. If someone tells you to 'snap out of it', remember that your wounds are merely reflecting back to them their own – so shower them in unconditional love and healing.

Rest in a place where you feel most peaceful. Take the time to feel and listen to your heart. Talk to your loved ones, tell them how much you care. Though you miss them, they're always around you, with your angels and spirit guides, eager to fill your heart with healing light.

Courage

EVEN THOUGH YOU MAY BE DELICATE,
YOU ARE STILL STRONG.
EMBRACE YOUR GENTLE SIDE
AND YOUR VULNERABILITY.
IT WILL ALLOW YOU TO SEE
THE GENTLENESS IN OTHERS.
IF YOU CAN BE VULNERABLE,
YOU DON'T NEED TO HIDE.

Focus on your journey, for you have a long way to travel. You may face struggles and battles – and at times, you may feel broken and weak, delicate and small... but you also have the power to be resilient, brave and unrelenting.

You will continue to evolve, always changing and shifting into new form. As a snake sheds its skin, you'll leave certain events, habits, people and environments behind. You will become surrounded by newness, as if donning a new cloak.

Take courage. Know that this new cloak will fit you perfectly. Even the darkest shades can reflect a dim light of their own. Don't be discouraged. Take a breath. Inhabit the present and before long, the dark shades will grow lighter, and you can shine once again.

Patience

WE LIVE IN A BUSY WORLD.
WE RUSH TOWARD A DESTINATION,
SOMETIMES USING FORCE AND
WILL TO MAKE THINGS HAPPEN.
WORKING IN THIS WAY
BLINDS YOU TO THE
WONDERFUL OPPORTUNITIES
THAT ORGANICALLY UNFOLD
THROUGH DIVINE TIMING.
FIRST BREATHE. WATCH. LISTEN.
THEN ACT!

Sometimes we can be so eager for the next phase of our journey, that we forget to stop and enjoy the moment. Focus your attention on right here, and right now. Know that everything will unfold as it's meant for you.

Do not allow impatience to creep in. Enjoy the journey just as much as the outcome, and explore your creativity, your passions and enthusiasm along the way.

Remember, Spirit has no concept of time – and while your guides are supporting you, timeframes also depend on others making choices that synchronise with yours.

When your will overrides those signposts and signals, it's easy to stop paying attention. Instead, take the time to tune into your feelings. Observe your dreams, and look for the signs – whether from animals, plants and nature, or billboards on the back of buses!

Life is not a race – and the deadlines we burden ourselves with are often ego-driven, and about making ourselves feel more worthy.

You already are enough! Slow down, and enjoy the journey.

Community

THERE IS A COLLECTIVE POWER OF MANY. EMBRACE THE SUPPORT NETWORK AROUND YOU. CONNECT WITH LIKEMINDED SOULS. SHARE YOUR DREAMS AND WATCH THEM FLOURISH TOGETHER!

Everything in our world is interconnected. Living things support one another – but sometimes, the thoughts and energies of others can be overwhelming. You may feel pulled left, right and centre by the opinions and judgements of those around you.

When you stand in your own truth, and value your own worth, there's less need to take on the opinions of others. Yet don't close off and cloister yourself, for this only limits the flow of shared ideas and the strength you'll find in community.

The power of many can make light work of even the hardest of tasks. Others may have special skills to help your project shine even more brightly. Perhaps these people have been drawn to you for a reason. Perhaps your special skills can in turn assist them. Reach out, connect, and exchange your truths with theirs – then watch your world expand, and the magic flow.

Romance

WE DO NOT ALWAYS
NEED ANOTHER
TO FEEL THAT GIDDY
FEELING OF ROMANCE.
BE ROMANTIC WITH YOURSELF.
TREAT YOURSELF TO
FLOWERS, SCENTED BATHS
AND BEAUTIFUL THOUGHTS.
YOU ARE WORTH IT!

Romance is not just about Valentines Day, and it's not even about another specific person in your life. Romance is about appreciation, and about demonstrating your love to the world.

A simple gesture – whether a smile, a compliment, or a flower to a random stranger – can melt a heart on any day of the year. The more you warm your heart and emit love energy, the more it will return to you, and envelop you like a favourite blanket. And while random acts of kindness to strangers can perpetuate this warm feeling of love, please remember to direct kindness and appreciation to yourself as well.

There is so much love to go around. You are an overflowing vessel, and there's no need to be frugal with love for yourself.

You are worth it!

Vulnerability

YOU DON'T ALWAYS NEED
TO SHOW YOUR SPIKES
TO SHIELD YOUR TENDER SIDE.
IF YOUR HEART IS OPEN,
AND YOU ARE ACCEPTING
OF YOURSELF
AND OTHERS,
YOU WILL BEGIN TO FEEL
STRONG AND SECURE,
EVEN THROUGH YOUR
VULNERABILITY.

Feeling vulnerable can be the strangest thing. It makes us feel raw, delicate and fragile. In this state, we can feel our heartache strongly. We feel like we can be broken so easily.

Others may tell us that we are far too open, that we need to protect ourselves, so that others may not prey on our vulnerability. Yet the more we take ownership of our vulnerability, the more we honour it, the stronger we become. As spiritual beings, we need to filter the energy that flows toward us, letting the positive come forth, whilst deflecting the negative – yet without closing ourselves off and creating more imbalance.

With an open heart, we can see the good in all. We can appreciate the beauty in the good, and even the not-so-good. With this knowingness, we can step forward into the world with our hearts open and our vulnerability intact, knowing that in remaining true to ourselves, we're stronger still.

Innocence

FOR MANY OF US,
CHILDHOOD WAS A MAGICAL TIME.
FAIRIES. SANTA. THE
EASTER BUNNY.
EVERYTHING SPARKLED
AND GLISTENED.
TAKE THE TIME TO REKINDLE
THAT INNOCENCE.
LOOK FOR THE FAIRIES – BOTH
IN THIS PICTURE, AND THE
WORLD AT LARGE.

'Stop daydreaming and step into the real world', some may say. I heard this often, particularly as a child, and also when studying metaphysics and energy. I would spend a lot of time in meditation and was often ungrounded, non-functional and neglectful of self. Yet after that had shifted, I realised the importance of fairy magic and innocence for my emotional wellbeing.

Today I live in a part of the world where wild fallow deer sometimes roam the hills. While I've never seen them in person, they venture onto our property at night, and I hear their throaty, haunting calls. This experience rekindles the magic of my childhood, filling me with a sense of wide-eyed wonder, excitement and anticipation.

Innocence and playfulness enlightens our spirit. It's like a holiday from the mundane. Take the time to play with your children or pets. Go fairy-spotting in the garden, or search for those fallow deer in the woods. It may be just the tonic you need to believe in magic once more.

Compassion

IMAGINE YOURSELF IN SOMEONE ELSE'S PREDICAMENT.
HOW WOULD YOU FEEL AND RESPOND?
SEND THEM UNCONDITIONAL LOVE AND LOTS OF HEALING LIGHT.

Often we become so engrossed in our own reality that we don't stop and think how our own lives are interwoven with the lives of others.

We're like comets on a collision course with each other, exploding at the point of impact. We may be hurt or angry at the way others behave. We might believe the other person is 'acting out' at us. We slip into victim mode.

Remember, another person's mood, actions or situation is rarely about you. If we can learn the lessons that confront us without judgement – and if we can peacefully reflect on what each moment shows us about our own journey – we can experience a new sense of oneness.

When we become increasingly familiar with this feeling of unconditional love and unity, we can continue along our path with more love and peace in our hearts – both for ourselves and others.

Change

THROUGHOUT OUR JOURNEY,
WE CONSTANTLY CHANGE
AND EVOLVE.
THE FORM WE STARTED LIFE WITH
DEVELOPS INTO THE
PERSON WE ARE TODAY,
SHAPED BY OUR LIFE-LESSONS
AND EXPERIENCES.
CHANGE IS A NATURAL PART OF LIFE.
NO TWO JOURNEYS ARE THE SAME,
AND ALL ARE EQUALLY AS VALUABLE
AS WE LEARN FROM
ANOTHER'S EXPERIENCES.

'A change is as good as a holiday', is something we so often hear. Consider how when we're on holiday, those unusual sights, sounds, smells and languages can add a new vibrancy to our experience. What if we were to always approach change as a holiday from the norm? Would we dread the disruptions to our patterns and lives quite so much?

New ideas and perspectives, an appreciation of individuality – they bring forth previously unforeseen opportunities. Know that you are being guided and shown the way forward at all times. Your intuition is always available to show you the way. It's just a matter of whether you listen and take heed – and it's this which determines the path you choose to travel.

Often when we travel to foreign lands, and immerse ourselves in unfamiliar cultures, we're prompted to make changes to the way we act and view life. We're inspired to embrace new ideals and perceptions. Change sparks an even greater inner journey – and it's something we should never fear, or shy away from.

Breathe

SOMETIMES LIFE IS A WHIRLWIND.
WE RUSH AROUND SO MUCH
WE FORGET TO BREATHE.
SLOW DOWN!

Life can move so quickly around us. Sometimes it feels like there's never enough time in the day to accomplish everything. Our packed calendars allow no room for flexibility or fluidity.

Take a breath, take a step back, and ground yourself. Imagine you're a tree, with roots growing down into the earth. Travel deeper and deeper, until you reach a pool of pink light, the colour of fairy floss. As you inhale, draw this light up into your legs, all the way up to the top of your head, as though you're a human straw. As you exhale, imagine that pink light moving out around your body.

This pink light represents unconditional love, and this is what you need to bathe in right now. You've been prioritising everyone else's needs ahead of your own, and you've forgotten to breathe.

Let the pink light wrap around you like a comforting blanket. Are you afraid of losing control? Are you afraid of letting others down? Fear is driving your reality. Yet deep down, understand that fear is just 'False Expectation Appearing Real'.

Observe the tasks causing you anxiety. Is your anxiety being caused by another? Are you taking on another's responsibility because you care for them? Is that person able to take it back? Then unburden yourself!

Are you able to reschedule? Can you rebalance your commitments? Please stop placing yourself last. Onus and responsibility is a shared reality. Breathe, take stock and self-nurture.

Acceptance

THERE IS BEAUTY IN BOTH
IMPERFECTION AND SIMPLICITY.
IF YOU STOP, TAKE A BREATH
AND THE TIME TO LOOK
YOU WILL BEGIN TO
APPRECIATE YOURSELF
AND THE WORLD AROUND YOU.
IN WHATEVER FORM IT
PRESENTS ITSELF.

I accept you for who you are, exactly as you are. When I see you, I don't see your imperfections. I don't want to fix you or change you. I see your beauty, your gentleness and your soul essence. I see how gifted you are. I admire you.

Each of us has our own set of unique qualities that make us who we are. When we're drawn to another person, we are often drawn to the qualities we'd subconsciously like to develop within ourselves.

Sometimes, people are numb to who they are on the inside. They only look outwards, for the approval of others. They focus on the imperfections of others, because they're actually looking into a mirror, and don't like what they see.

Stay true to yourself. Keep your heart open and show unconditional love toward those people, even in the face of their criticism – for they are trapped in their own pain.

Possession

APPRECIATE THE WORLD
AROUND YOU.
THERE'S BEAUTY EVERYWHERE.
IT MAY VARY.
IT MAY BE TRANSFORMATIVE.
THERE'S NO NEED TO OWN IT.
APPRECIATE BEAUTY
IN WHATEVER FORM IT
PRESENTS ITSELF.

Holding on to things that aren't ours to keep is something we humans do quite a bit. We give energy to certain people, situations and things that essentially close us off to other, more valuable opportunities. Yet if we can let go of expectation, and just acknowledge and observe, we can more easily accept a situation for what it is.

Possession of ideals and objects holds us in a pattern of stasis. Like a body of water, we need to be able to move with the current, so we can be guided toward new opportunities not previously considered. Holding on hard to objects and ideals, we limit ourselves – and just like water that's unable to move with the current, stagnation results.

Loving, and being loved does not always need to be an outward projection. If you love yourself, and treat yourself as your own heart's desire, you'll begin to emit a higher vibration of love and acceptance. The Universal Law of Attraction flows, enabling like-minded others to be more readily drawn to you. You'll enjoy more choice, and greater freedom to choose what you want from your life. You become more available for the flow of new ideas and opportunities. Let go of the 'fear of lack', and you'll receive more than you could ever dream of.

Support

SUPPORT IS AVAILABLE FROM FAMILY, FRIENDS AND THE COMMUNITY AROUND YOU. DON'T CLOSE YOURSELF OFF. THEIR LOVE AND ACCEPTANCE WILL LIFT AND SUPPORT YOU.

Everything in our Universe is interconnected. In every eco-system, one set of molecules relies on another set for survival. Every plant and animal exists for a reason. Each being has a path, and a unique destiny to follow.

You are not alone. You have your own ecosystem of support, even if it may not always feel that way. Sometimes we can imagine that support needs to come from a particular source – and we try to force it, or pine after it, becoming hurt and angry when things don't go our way.

When we can sit and quieten our mental noise, taking the time to absorb the abundant beauty around us, we can begin to perceive situations differently. Insights enter our awareness. 'Ah-ha' moments transform our perspective. Messages begin to appear, whether in books we read, words from a stranger, signs on the street or insights from nature.

Do you keep seeing particular animals or birds? What are they doing? What do these animals represent to you? When you are able to take in these types of messages, you begin to realise how much support is actually around you.

Purity

As winter begins to wane,
new hope emerges.
Hope which is pure in
intent and focus.
Pure of heart.
Focus on the future,
not on the past.
Time to put your best
foot forward.

Be pure of heart, and pure of intent. The key to happiness is in learning to be true to yourself, and in stepping into your own personal spotlight. Own your past lessons and learn from them, and you can more easily accept who you are, and where you've come from.

Open your heart to yourself, and love yourself for how much you've grown. Know that the journey and process of development is eternal. Be at peace. With an open heart, new growth and flourishing is inevitable, and when you're able to accept your own journey, you can more easily inspire and assist others in their own.

Stand in your light, with your big, beautiful open heart, and your actions will only ever come from love, and with the the best interests of those around you. The real magic is that the more you inhabit this role, the more you'll attract others who behave the same.

Go forth and weave your matrix of unconditional love, and then revel in its simplicity, its purity and its gifts.

Excitement

When you feel those tingling sensations of excitement, an opportunity has manifested for you. Something positive. Own it. Enjoy it. Follow your heart, and explore where it takes you.

The feeling of excitement is like a palette of vivid paint colours, waiting for you to conjure a picture in whatever hues you choose.

These feelings are precious jewels, glistening and sparkling in anticipation of the experience about to unfold. When an opportunity lands on your path effortlessly and without force, you know it's meant to be. Trust that you will be guided where you need to go.

The magic may wane sometimes. This is natural – especially during times of rapid growth. When you experience struggle and pain, sometimes a change might be necessary. This may not always mean a change in circumstance. It could be as simple nurturing a neglected aspect of yourself, releasing an old habit, or developing a new one that better supports your health and wellbeing.

Joy

FOLLOWING YOUR HAPPINESS
LEADS YOU TO THE CORE OF YOUR
SPIRIT AND YOUR LIFE'S PURPOSE.
TRUST IN YOURSELF
AND WHAT YOU HAVE TO OFFER.
IGNITE YOUR PASSION!

When we are on the right path, joy is a magical life force that bubbles up to the surface. Everything flows, everything is love. And when we can stand in our light, and effuse who we really are out into the ether, those with compatible interests are drawn near.

You need to trust in yourself and your capabilities, for you are far more talented than you give yourself credit for. When you live your truth and follow your dreams with every fibre of your being, your joy can burn bright like a flame.

It takes courage to stand in your truth, to be open and honest with who you are, as you are. Not everyone is going to accept you, or relate to your passions. However, know that the Universal Law of Attraction is at play.

The road may be bumpy, and you may be tested. Some may try to dissuade you from pursuing your goal. Trust in yourself. Break down the goal into smaller tasks, and bit by bit, work towards your end game.

Some of you may not yet know what your life's purpose is . You may feel like you've have dabbled in so much, scattering your energies here and there, but nothing has really inspired you. It's time to just be still. Slow down and focus your energies. Spend some quiet time on your own, and meditate on what stirs you, on what grabs your attention.

Please remember that to truly appreciate joy, sometimes you need to be sorrowful. You would take joy for granted otherwise. However, sorrow will inspire you to embrace your joy even more.

Don't stay in sorrow for long. Simply acknowledge it, then focus on appreciating what's beautiful – for that beauty is waiting to lead you back to your natural state of JOY!

Strength

YOU MAY HAVE BEEN
CUT OFF OR HURT,
BUT IN TIME, HEALING
WILL TAKE PLACE,
AND NEW SUSTAINABLE
GROWTH BEGINS.

Sometimes, when our progress is halted, and our ego is pruned, we can be left feeling vulnerable and weak. Our pride becomes wounded, and we're left in limbo, unsure of our next move.

For those of us who gain security from always controlling, foreseeing and planning our next step, the unknown is frightening and unnerving. Go with the flow. A new beginning, no matter how mysterious, offers choices and opportunities you may not previously have considered.

Even when the pruning is savage, it can lead to stronger re-growth later, and a more resilient structure. Know that you will come through any adversity stronger and more powerful than you've ever been before.

Adversity

EVEN IN THE WORST OF CIRCUMSTANCES BEAUTY, LOVE AND HOPE CAN EMERGE. DON'T GIVE UP!

During our lifetimes, we have many obstacles and challenges to overcome. Some of those challenges we can believe ourselves too weak to overcome. Trust and focus is required. With determination, you will overcome what lies in your path.

I trained competitively as a shot put and discus thrower, competing at club and state level – and as a part of my training, I would visualise the achievement of my goal distances. By the time competition day arrived, 'throwing the distance' was a matter of routine.

This is the Universal Law of Attraction at work – and we can utilise this technique in every aspect of our lives. Wherever fear plays a part (and for many of us, it's often the main obstacle), keep in mind that fear is merely a false illusion imposed by our imagination.

One way to keep fear at bay so we can move forward on our path, is to imagine that our fears are like Pac-Man characters, and that we can obliterate them by simply charging through them. Remember that to a large extent, we are each in control of our destiny, because we have freedom to choose how to respond to any event or circumstance.

Growth occurs even in the most impossible of circumstances – and just like the tulip that blooms from end of an old ceramic sewer pipe, so too can you flourish under the most challenging conditions.

Harmony

EACH OF US HAS A PART TO PLAY IN THIS THEATRE CALLED LIFE.

EACH OF US BRINGS STRENGTHS, IDEAS, INSPIRATIONS AND GIFTS TO THE COMMUNITY.

TOGETHER WE CREATE MAGIC!

Every living thing is interlinked and interwoven. Each molecule relies on one another for survival and success. Naturally, we all work together to achieve a greater good. We each have our set of strengths and weaknesses that complements those of others.

When we're where we need to be, we experience feelings of elation, joy and peace. Conversely, feelings of discord, frustration and anger are signs that we still have lesson to learn in order to grow. Discord can be a sign that change needs to happen, or that you still need to adjust to a change that's already occurred.

A symphony orchestra playing the sweetest lilt embraces light and shade. When musicians play together, entranced by their passion for music, the delicate balance takes you, the listener, on a magical journey, as if you are floating along a river. Beauty is manifested. There is no struggle, no pain, no frustration nor anger. Infectious peace, love and joy wells up, and multiplies in abundance, gathering size, momentum and a power that can move mountains with emotion. Harmony is an unstoppable force, touching all who stand in its path.

When we are enthralled by our bliss, time is irrelevant. Everything is easy. Struggle dissipates, and life flows. When we are in this place, we feel at one with the universe.

Rejuvenate

YOU MAY BE FEELING
A LITTLE WORSE FOR WEAR,
A LITTLE BEDRAGGLED
AND WORN OUT.
NOW IS THE TIME TO REPLENISH.

When we're feeling depleted and bedraggled, this is a sign that we're perhaps not showing ourselves the due care we deserve.

Nourish yourself, take the rest you need, and prepare yourself for the journey ahead. You are worthy – and you should be placing yourself at the top of the queue when it comes to looking after yourself, rather than putting everyone else ahead of you.

Remember, you'll be more capable of working to your true potential when your petrol tank is full!

Power

SOMETIMES WHEN WE'RE ALONE,
WE FEEL SO SMALL AND POWERLESS.
YET ONE TINY MOLECULE
HAS THE POWER
TO CREATE CHANGE
ON A MASSIVE SCALE.

Power struggles can occur physically, verbally, visually and energetically. Often, we feel power struggles most keenly when they appear in relation to others. Perhaps another wants you to act in a certain way, yet you want a different outcome. Imagine a game of tug of war. The opposing team pulls one way, trying to coerce you. You pull back the other way, wanting the opposite. They get angry and tug harder, and in response, and you do the same.

But what if you were to stop reacting? What if you stood quietly in your personal power, not moving or responding to their attempts? What if you were to calmly say 'no' to their demands. What if you simply let go of the rope?

When you can stand in your personal power, you don't need to fight to be heard. You are able to just stand confidently and quietly, deflecting those trying to gain leverage. You are able to calmly state your truth, and you are able to walk away from anyone attempting to twist and weave your words against you.

What anyone else says and thinks about you is none of your business! It's simply a mirror for whatever that person is dealing with internally. Show them compassion. Words are powerful! Words can hurt and words can heal. Choose your words carefully and with healing intent, for the highest good.

It can sometimes be difficult to deflect the negative energy of others. To help you maintain a calm, confident demeanour, and also protect yourself energetically, imagine a beam of gold light around your auric field (the region encircling your body), and then visualise a mirror reflecting back any negative energy to wherever it came from.

Love

AN OPEN HEART EMPOWERS AN OPEN MIND.
THE LOVE YOU SEEK IS ALL AROUND YOU.
GO WITH THE FLOW.

Most of us are born into love, but we grow seeking love as though it is no longer around us. We seek love and approval from parents, trying to win their acceptance. We seek love and acceptance from friends, and even from strangers. When did love become so conditional?

Our culture of judging and using love as a carrot on a stick has blinded us to the fact that there is a deep pool of unconditional love within ourselves. If we draw on this pool, we have the capacity to experience love at all times, without limitation.

We buy into our 'judgment and acceptance' culture because that is what we're taught by those who have not yet taken the dive into the unconditional love pool.

Time to go swimming!

Abundance

YOU SOWED YOUR
SEEDS OF EFFORT.
YOU NURTURED
THIS GARDEN
OF INSPIRATION.
PREPARE FOR YOUR
BOUNTIFUL HARVEST.
ALL YOUR HARD WORK
IS ABOUT TO PAY OFF.

There is so much love around you. So often we believe we don't have enough love in our lives – not enough energy, money, luck or blessings. We view life through the eyes of 'lack' – and yet, our lives are actually quite full. We don't see it, because we are so busy concentrating on what we don't have.

Like attracts like – so to kick-start your abundant frame of mind, act and talk like you already all have money, the luck and the blessings you desire, and you'll start to experience some shifts.

Here's a quick visualisation exercise to help you feel the unconditional love that's always available to you.

Imagine a column of white light coming down from the Universe and entering the top of your head, travelling down your spine, into your legs and through your feet into the ground beneath you. Imagine the white light travelling deep into the earth until it reaches a pool of pale pink light.

As you inhale, draw that pale pink light up into your body. As you exhale, feel that pale pink light fill your heart and move out into your auric field.

Now imagine the pink light cycling in through the back and out through the front of your heart chakra. See this pink light cleansing your heart, allowing room for greater love. Feel your heart becoming warm and full.

With regard to money, thank the Universe for already working toward your financial goal. Ask to be guided, to be shown how you can assist this manifestation. Explore whether there might be another thought pattern or habit that's holding you back. Take responsibility for what you contribute energetically to the world. Plan for success and abundance.

Balance

TIME TO NURTURE
YOURSELF AND OTHERS.
BE GENTLE.
SEEK A WORLD OF HARMONY
AND BALANCE.
TRUST THAT YOU'LL FIND
THAT EQUILIBRIUM
WITHIN.

Balance is required in all things. Whether it's light and shade, or colour and texture, balance is a central governing force. Even in regards to the things we label 'good' or 'bad', balance is required, so we can appreciate both ends of the continuum.

Balance in work and play is also key to our wellbeing. Take the time to focus on your wellness and your inner equilibrium, for it will help you to prosper on all levels.

The geranium is a flower that aptly symbolises balance. Its chemical composition promotes hormonal balance, and assists in our physical, mental and emotional wellbeing.

Celebrate

WHY PUT OFF CELEBRATIONS
UNTIL TOMORROW,
WHEN YOU CAN EXPERIENCE
THE JOY AND EXCITEMENT TODAY.
YOU ARE BLESSED
TO BE SURROUNDED
BY SUCH ABUNDANCE.

Celebrate even the small things in your life. Don't just wait for the grander plans to manifest. The more you generate an energy of celebration, the more opportunities for celebration you will attract.

Celebrate your body with dance and good food. Celebrate those special to you with warm thoughts and gestures. Celebrate the beauty of nature by taking the time to appreciate it.

Celebrate other people's successes. Feel their joy and excitement as if it were your own. Celebrate your uniqueness by not hiding it under a bushel, for fear of judgment. Stand proud and wear your uniqueness like a badge of honour, for it is what makes you special.

Honour and celebrate yourself, and honour and celebrate others. In turn, they'll do the same for you!

Cleanse

NOW IS THE TIME TO CLEANSE YOUR LIFE. LET GO OF ANYTHING THAT NO LONGER SERVES YOU. IF YOU ARE FEELING WEIGHED DOWN, SWAPPING NEW HABITS FOR OLD MAY BRIGHTEN YOUR SPIRITS!

We can use and abuse our bodies quite readily – often without considering their requirements for daily care. We're so busy that we fuel ourselves with whatever's convenient, or what we're told to eat, rather than taking a moment to acknowledge our more fundamental nutritional needs.

Now's the time to start paying attention to your body, so it can serve you as it's meant to. Take a step back, begin a cleanse, and replenish with what your body really needs. This is also a good time to consult a health practitioner, to assist you on your cleansing path.

Take the opportunity to also purify your thoughts and actions. Reflect on what you need to work on, and devise an appropriate plan of action.

You stand at a crossroads, on a precipice of a great journey. Now's the time to prepare, cleanse and grow strong.

Guidance

FOCUS YOUR ENERGIES
ON WHAT YOU REALLY, REALLY,
REALLY WANT TO DO IN LIFE.
TAKE THE TIME TO ENJOY
THE JOURNEY.
TRUST THAT YOU WILL BE GUIDED
TOWARD THE PATH YOU
NEED TO TAKE.
TAKE CHARGE OF YOUR CHOICES.

How often have you felt a presence, had a feeling in your gut, or heard words in your head that have been so potent, they've prompted you to act?

Now's the time to trust your instincts and place faith in your impulses – particularly if they're driven by your heart space. They will take you exactly where you need to be.

Focus

CLOSE YOUR EYES FOR A MOMENT.
FOCUS ON YOUR BREATH.
INHALE FOR A COUNT OF THREE,
THEN RELEASE YOUR BREATH.
OPEN YOUR EYES
AND
LOOK INTO THE CENTRE
OF THE FLOWER.
ASK YOURSELF
WHAT YOU NEED TO
FOCUS ON FOR TODAY.

Clear your mind of distractions. Acknowledge any thoughts that come into your mind, then inform your ego that you'll address these intruding thoughts later. Sit quietly for just a few moments and focus on your breathing.

Then open your eyes and look deeply into the centre of this flower.

Make a list of the tasks you need to tackle to help you achieve your goal. Prepare yourself for the journey ahead. Be in the present moment and address each task as if it were a stepping stone on your path to success.

Judgement

THERE IS BEAUTY AND
WORTH IN EVERY BEING.
MANY PEOPLE SEE THE BEAUTY
IN WHAT OTHERS
DEEM UNSIGHTLY.
DO NOT BE DISHEARTENED
BY ANOTHER'S
JUDGEMENT OF YOU.

Everyone has an opinion, and that is okay. Opinions are vehicles through which we articulate life experience. They are a vital and necessary part of all of us.

Yet another's opinion has nothing to do with you – even when that expression is aimed right at you. Remember, opinions are merely a reflection of another's individual journey. We don't see the world as it is. We see the world as we are.

It's a fruitless exercise to stay small in a bid to avoid the judgement of others. Nothing is gained – and in many respects, something is lost – because the world misses out on who you really are.

You have so much to contribute to the world. Stand bold, and don't limit yourself for fear of the judgement of others.

Believe

Believe in yourself.
Believe in your intuition.
Believe you are worthy.
Believe in the goodness
of others.
Believe in miracles.
Believe in Spirit!

When you believe in yourself, the innate goodness of others, and the possibility for miracles, you attract more of everything good and true in your life.

Each of us comes into this life with our own special gifts. Trust that you are worthy and capable of expressing these gifts. You are capable and worthy. You merely need to be you, just as you are.

Passion

TO FIND WHAT MAKES YOU 'TICK'
MANY SAY THAT THE KEY IS IN
DOING WHAT YOU ENJOY
AND
ENJOYING WHAT YOU DO
THERE WILL ALWAYS BE LESS
ENJOYABLE CHORES...
BUT THE END GOAL AND RESULT
MAKES IT ALL WORTHWHILE!

What is your passion? What really cranks your tractor?!

To be passionate is to care, and to live life fully. Passion comes from great presence, from the savouring of experience. Passion is the pathway to purpose.

Don't allow the judgement of others to influence your passion. Fear of judgement stunts your growth and creativity.

Be engaged with the world around you. Spend time doing what you enjoy. Create. Manifest. Enjoy!

Grounding

WITH SO MUCH GOING
ON IN OUR LIVES,
WE CAN FEEL LIKE WE
ARE BEING PULLED
IN MANY DIRECTIONS
SIMULTANEOUSLY.
WE FEEL SCATTERED.
WE CANNOT COMPLETE
THE PROJECTS WE START.
TAKE A BREATH. CLOSE YOUR EYES.
IMAGINE YOU ARE A
TREE WITH ROOTS
GROWING DEEP INTO THE EARTH.
NOW OPEN YOUR EYES
AND PROCEED!

When our energies are scattered, we forget things. We take shortcuts. We exhaust our bodies and minds. We become burnt out.

To make the most of our lives on earth, we need to be grounded enough to integrate guidance into physical manifestation.

'Witness consciousness' is required here. Become aware of your thoughts, your actions, your feelings and your body. Take a deep breath. Focus on your surroundings. Be mindful of how you wish to proceed.

Understand that you are the conduit between heaven and earth. Spiritual endeavours are wonderful things – and earthbound endeavours, sparked by spiritual or divine guidance, are nothing short of magical.

The Secret To Reading The Images

Preparation

Before undertaking an image reading, take a moment to centre yourself. Close your eyes and focus on your breathing. Inhale for a count of three, release and repeat.

Imagine a column of white light coming down from the Universe and entering the top of your head. Imagine that white light travelling down your spine as you inhale. Imagine that white light moving down into your feet, into the earth, and then travelling deep down, until it reaches a pool of pink light.

As you inhale, draw this pink light up through the earth into the soles of your feet – almost as though you're a human straw! As you exhale, imagine the pink light moving out around your physical body and enveloping you like a warm, pink, fluffy blanket of unconditional love.

Ask to be aligned to your Higher Self. Request that your Higher Guidance steps closer, to support and assist.

Trust Your Intuition

While each image in this book is accompanied by inspirational writing, the meaning behind each photograph very much depends upon your own individual intuition. Here's how to access your intuition and 'read' each flower:

Look deeply into the image. What do you see? What part of the image holds your attention? Why do you feel that?

Now look at the colours. Which of them are the most vivid for you? (See below for more guidance on colours).

What types of feelings do you get when you look at the image?

Again, look deeply into the flower or plant. Ask to be shown the message this particular flower can offer you. Write it down.

Don't second-guess the information you receive from the photographs. Just write it down as you receive it. And don't judge it!

Significance Of Colours

Many years ago, while studying Metaphysics at Chiara College in Sydney, we had to live for a week at a time immersed in each of the seven primary colours.

While undertaking this weekly exercise, I was astounded by the thoughts, emotions and dynamics that manifested when surrounding myself with each of the colours. This practice highlighted the chakras I personally had the most difficulty with, guiding me with what I needed to work on to achieve a better energetic balance.

Each colour along the spectrum resonates with a primary chakra in the energetic body or auric field. These chakra structures are like spinning wheels through which we take in energy from the outside world and assimilate it, providing insights into what's happening around us vibrationally.

Chakra	Colour	Meaning:
Base	Red	Survival. Money. Stability. Security.
Sacral	Orange	Creativity. Emotions. Fear. Sexual Energy.
Solar Pexus	Yellow	Power. Self-confidence. Self-worth. Control.
Heart	Green	Love.
Throat	Blue	Communication. Relating.
Brow	Indigo	Perception. Judgement.
Crown	Violet	Spiritual Connection.

About The Author

Anne McCormack first discovered her passion for Natural Therapies 26 years ago. After being awarded a Diploma in Aromatherapy from NSW Academy of Clinical Aromatherapy and a Diploma in Remedial Massage with Nature Care College in Sydney, Anne worked in a number of successful healing clinics around Sydney.

During her time working as an Aromatherapist and Remedial Massage Therapist, Anne became aware of her ability to feel the pain and emotions of others. On mentioning this strange revelation to a medium, she visited Chatswood Spiritualist Church, where the development of her mediumship abilities flourished.

Anne's personal journey led her to studying Metaphysics and Parapsychology with Chiara College. Her Aromatherapy and Remedial Massage repertoire grew to include chakra balancing, guided meditations, and even a gig as an in-store tarot reader.

Anne has presented workshops and been a guest speaker for the New South Wales YWCA Encore Group for women coping with breast cancer. She has also conducted workshops on chakra and auric awareness for the Australian Acting Academy in Brisbane (Australia).

These days, Anne resides in sunny Nelson, a piece of paradise at the top of the New Zealand's South Island, where she discovered a passion for nature photography, which quickly became another vehicle for facilitating the healing process in those around her.

Leading a very busy life, photography made Anne stop and take notice of the world around her, and is something that has provided her with so much peace during challenging times.

Other Publications By Anne McCormack

Lovitude: Trying To Calm The Monkey Mind
ISBN: 978-0-473-37321-4

Sometimes, when you are going through a rough patch in your life, all you need is a hug, and a holiday from your head. You will find both inside this book.

Reviews

"Your book Lovitude was a really positive reading experience. Once I started I just sat and kept reading. It made me take time to stop and refocus on the little things. Looking at all your beautiful photos, and thinking wow what a beautiful world you live in!! Then I realised a few of the photos are from where I still live, and yes they are beautiful too. I do live in a beautiful place, and have now decided to take time to stop, look, listen, smell and feel what is around me and not just rush, rush, rush all the time. Just sitting at the beach now is a different experience. The other day while Jade was playing, I closed my eyes and listened to to noises around me, while the wind was blowing on my face, and took some deep breaths - it was beautiful."
— Tanya K, Adelaide (South Australia)

"I recently purchased 2 copies of Lovitude, 1 for myself and 1 as a gift. Lovitude is a beautiful book with stunning photographs. Anne has a special talent for photography and has written some lovely words that help us to reflect on what is important in life and how to find that calm, inner peace. If you need a gift for someone who has everything, or may be going through a tough time, then this is perfect."
— Sharon A, Adelaide (South Australia)

CPSIA information can be obtained
at www.ICGtesting.com
Printed in the USA
BVOW05s1140150817
5853BVAU00002B/4/P

9 781504 307765

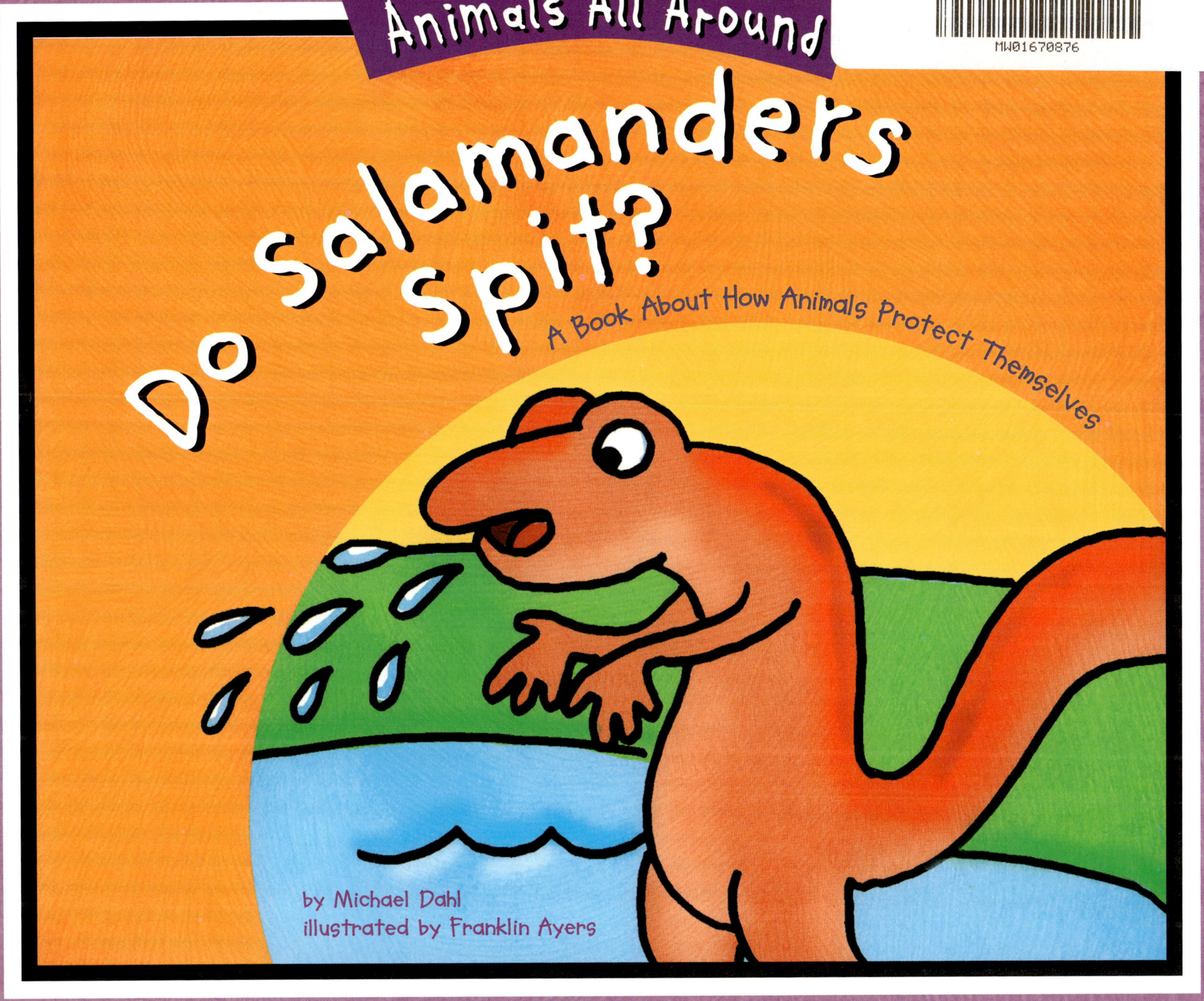

Special thanks to our advisers for their expertise:

Kathleen E. Hunt, Ph.D.
Research Scientist & Lecturer, Zoology Department
University of Washington, Seattle, Washington

Susan Kesselring, M.A., Literacy Educator
Rosemount-Apple Valley-Eagan (Minnesota) School District

PICTURE WINDOW BOOKS
MINNEAPOLIS, MINNESOTA

Managing Editor: Bob Temple
Creative Director: Terri Foley
Editor: Peggy Henrikson
Editorial Adviser: Andrea Cascardi
Copy Editor: Laurie Kahn
Designer: Todd Ouren
Page production: BANTA Digital Group
The illustrations in this book were rendered digitally.

Picture Window Books
5115 Excelsior Boulevard
Suite 232
Minneapolis, MN 55416
1-877-845-8392
www.picturewindowbooks.com

Printed in the United States of America.

Library of Congress Cataloging-in-Publication Data
Dahl, Michael.
Do salamanders spit? : a book about how animals protect themselves / by Michael Dahl ;
illustrated by Franklin Ayers.
p. cm. — (Animals all around)
Includes bibliographical references and index.
ISBN 1-4048-0291-6 (hardcover)
ISBN 1-4048-0380-7 (paperback)
1. Animal defenses—Juvenile literature. [1. Animal defenses.]
I. Ayers, Franklin, 1962- ill. II. Title.
QL759 .D33 2004
591.47—dc22
2003020115

Do salamanders spit?

No! Black cobras spit.

A frightened black spitting cobra raises its body and flares its hood. Then the cobra spits deadly poison called venom at its enemy's eyes. The venom can blind the cobra's enemy and save the snake.

Do salamanders use claws?

No! Jaguars use claws.

A jaguar has sharp claws to slash at dangerous enemies. When the cat is frightened, its claws slide smoothly and quickly out of its paws. Its claws also help the jaguar quickly climb trees to escape.

Do salamanders curl into balls?

No! Three-banded armadillos curl into balls.

The three-banded armadillo has a thick, bony covering. To protect itself from enemies, the armadillo rolls up into a tight ball. Its tough outer plates of armor fit together like a puzzle.
They completely cover the curled-up creature.

Do salamanders squirt ink?

No! Squid squirt ink.

Squid can swim swiftly in the sea. But faster, larger creatures like to eat squid. When a squid is threatened, it squirts ink into the water. The dark, inky cloud confuses the enemy. The hidden squid can slip safely away.

Do salamanders outrun enemies?

No! Jackrabbits outrun enemies.

A lean, long-legged jackrabbit can outrun humans and hunting dogs. It is faster than foxes and coyotes. With its powerful legs, the jackrabbit can escape a hungry mountain lion by leaping over the cat in a single bound.

Do salamanders puff up like spiky balloons?

No! Porcupine fish puff up like spiky balloons.

The porcupine fish has loose, stretchy skin. When surprised or attacked, the fish gulps in water and blows up like a balloon. Sharp spines pop out on its skin. This spiky ball scares away the fish's enemies.

Do salamanders shock?

No! Electric eels shock.

Slippery eels slide through the dark waters of South American rivers. If these snakelike fish are frightened, they will defend themselves with powerful electric shocks. Zap! Enemies are stunned and fall away.

Do salamanders disguise themselves as leaves?

No! Javanese leaf insects disguise themselves as leaves.

Green leaf insects live in the hot, wet jungles of Java. Like many other animals, leaf insects protect themselves with camouflage. Their flat green legs and bodies look like leaves, so they can hide from hungry birds.

Do salamanders hide in other creatures?

No! Clown fish hide in other creatures.

Clown fish hide in the waving tentacles of creatures called sea anemones. The anemone's stinging tentacles are poisonous to other animals. But the clown fish has special, slimy skin that protects it from the sting.

Do salamanders drop their tails?

Yes! Salamanders drop their tails.

Some salamanders have a sneaky way of escaping enemies. If a hungry raccoon tries to snatch the salamander—snap! The salamander's tail breaks off! The raccoon is left with the wiggling tail, and the salamander scoots to safety. Then it can grow a new tail.

How Animals Protect Themselves

Some animals flee and escape.

jackrabbits	outrun their enemies
salamanders	drop their tails and flee

Some animals change their bodies.

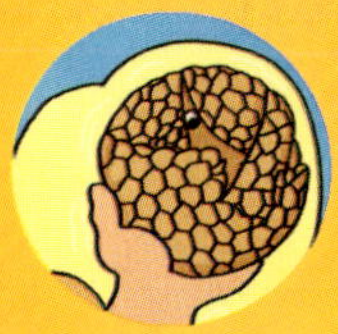

three-banded armadillos	curl into balls
porcupine fish	puff up like spiky balloons

Some animals have weapons.

black spitting cobras	spit venom
jaguars	use sharp claws

Some animals disguise themselves.

Javanese leaf insects	look like leaves

Some animals use special tricks.

squid	squirt ink
electric eels	shock
clown fish	hide in other creatures

Glossary

armor—a hard covering that protects the animal or person underneath

camouflage—special covering that helps animals, people, or objects blend in with their surroundings. A leaf insect uses both its green color and its leaf shape as camouflage.

disguise—to hide by looking like something else. The leaf insect disguises itself as a leaf with its color and shape.

electric shock—a jolt of electric energy. An electric shock can hurt or even kill an animal or a person.

hood—the wide, curving sides of a cobra's head that appear when the snake is frightened. The hood makes the cobra look bigger to scare its enemies.

sea anemone (uh-NEM-uh-nee)—a sea creature that looks something like a flower called an anemone

spine—a sharp, pointed growth

tentacle—a long, narrow body part. The sea anemone has many tentacles that wave in the currents of the ocean.

venom—poison

Index

To Learn More

At the Library

Ganeri, Anita. *Extraordinary Dangerous Animals*. New Scholastic, 2001.

Jenkins, Steve. *What Do You Do When Something Wa Eat You?* Boston: Houghton Mifflin, 1997.

Martin, James. *The Spitting Cobras of Africa*. Mank Minn.: Capstone Press, 1995.

Stone, Lynne M. *Sharp and Sticky Stuff*. Vero Beach, Rourke Press, 1996.

Taylor, Barbara. *Scary and Sneaky*. Chicago: Peter B Books, 2001.

On the Web

Fact Hound offers a safe, fun way to find Web sites related to this book. All of the sites on Fact Hound have been researched by our staff.
http://www.facthound.com

1. Visit the Fact Hound home page.
2. Enter a search word related to this book, or type in this special code: 1404802916.
3. Click on the FETCH IT button.

Your trusty Fact Hound will fetch the best sites for